MW00464462

This Book belongs to

....

....

Roses buttercream flower wreath cake

Ranunculus buttercream flower wreath cake

Cherry Blossom buttercream flower wreath cake

© OLGA ZAYTSEVA

Daffodils and Roses buttercream flower wreath cake

Ranunculus and Hydrangeas buttercream flower wreath cake

Water Lily buttercream flower cake

© OLGA ZAYTSEVA

English Roses buttercream flower wreath cake

© OLGA ZAYTSEVA

Roses and Hydrangeas buttercream flower clouds cake

Poppies buttercream flower wreath cake

Tulips buttercream flower wreath cake

 Camomile buttercream flower wreath cake

© OLGA ZAYTSEVA

Peonies and Poppies buttercream flower wreath cake

Chrysanthemums and Roses buttercream flower cloud cake

© OLGA ZAYTSEVA

 Dahlias and Roses buttercream flower bouquet cake

© OLGA ZAYTSEVA

Poppies buttercream flower wreath cake

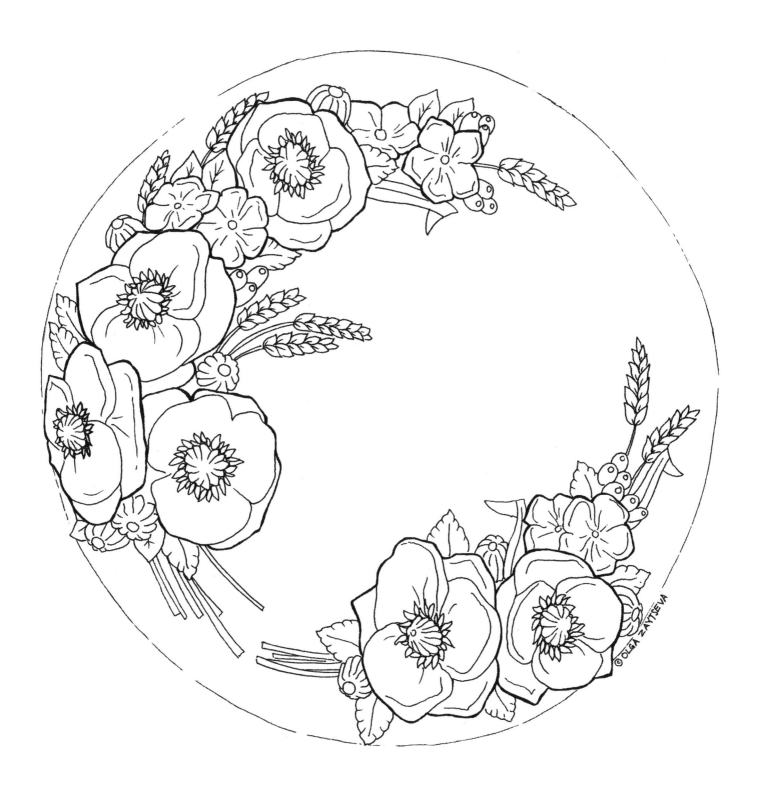

Roses and Chrysanthemums buttercream flower wreath cake

 Roses buttercream flower wreath cake

© OLGA ZAYTSEVA

Sunflowers, Roses and Chrysanthemums buttercream flower wreath cake

English Roses and Berries buttercream flower cake

© OLGA ZAYTSEVA

Zinnias and Pumpkins buttercream flower wreath cake

© OLGA ZAYTSEVA

Roses and Berries buttercream flower wreath cake

© OLGA ZAYTSEVA

Asters buttercream flower wreath cake

© OLGA ZAYTSEVA

 Roses and Berries buttercream flower wreath cake

© OLGA ZAYTSEVA

Valentine's Day buttercream flower cake

© OLGA ZAYTSEVA

Chrysanthemums and Berries buttercream flower wreath cake

© OLGA ZAYTSEVA

Roses and Berries buttercream flower cake

© OLGA ZAYTSEVA

 Poinsettia buttercream flower wreath cake

© OLGA ZAYTSEVA

Roses, Chrysanthemums and Pine cones buttercream flower wreath cake

© OLGA ZAYTSEVA

Calla Lilies and Roses heart shaped buttercream flower wreath cake

© OLGA ZAYTSEVA